Presentational Skills for the Next Generation

Presentational Skills for the Next Generation

Ginger Marks

DocUmeant Publishing
85 N Main St
Florida, NY 10921
Phone: 646-233-4366

Published by
DocUmeant Publishing
14 Wall St 20th Floor
NY, NY 10005

Phone: 646-233-4366

Cover Photographers
Emlyn Addison www.ixwa.com
Philip Marks
James Snell
http://www.morguefile.com/archive/?author=monosodium

Illustrations, Layout & Design: Ginger Marks
http://www.DocUmeantDesigns.com

Copy & Developmental Editors
Kim Mutch Emerson
http://www.writingpro.biz

Dawn Batterbee-Miller
http://www.DawnCreations.net

Deepak Morris
http://www.freewebs.com/deepakmorris/

Library of Congress Cataloging-in-Publication Data
Marks, Ginger
          Presentational Skills for the Next Generation: business, PowerPoint,
presentation, skills, teaching, instruction, design.
LCCN - 2011934331

First publishing date: 08/2006
Second edition: 10/2006
Third edition: 07/2011

ISBN# 978-0-9788831-4-0 14.95

Testimonials

Presentational Skills for the Next Generation covers a wide range of topics that presenters need to know. Some of the topics, such as organizing the content and working with audio-visual technology are rarely covered. The author's emphasis on rehearsing and considering the audience first are very valuable. You'll also find excellent coverage on the delivery aspect of presenting, including how to dress, what equipment to pack, dealing with fear, and more. The Resources section at the end is very useful, too."
Ellen Finkelstein
Presentation skills trainer and PowerPoint MVP

◆◆◆◆◆

"As a communication consultant and instructor of public speaking, I have taught hundreds of people how to prepare and deliver successful presentations. For anyone who has to give a presentation, I would definitely recommend *Presentational Skills for the Next Generation* by Ginger Marks. This easy-to-read book provides excellent ideas for putting together a polished presentation. Ginger's explanation on preparing and using visual aids to compliment your talk is especially well

done. Ginger covers all-important areas of preparing an effective presentation from considering your audience and the location of your talk to your personal appearance and valuable delivery tips and techniques. This book is a great resource that you can refer to time-and-again for every presentation you'll ever do."
Felicia J. Slattery, M.A., M.Ad.Ed.
Communication Consultant, Speaker & Coach

◆◆◆◆◆

"Ginger Marks has codified a very workable system of materials to help anyone who desires to be an improved presenter. The skills of presentation could be said to be an artful science and Ginger represents this concept very effectively in her latest work. *Presentation Skills for the Next Generation* is a very valuable must read."
Joe Yazbeck, Founder-President
Prestige Leader Development

◆◆◆◆◆

"I read through *Presentational Skills for the Next Generation* last night and thought it was great. My 'presentations' at my job are limited to one-on-one client meetings, but there are great tips in there that are beneficial for all kinds of presentations. Fantastic read!
Thanks again, I'll keep it close at hand!"
Holly Hixon
Account/Office Manager

◆◆◆◆◆

"Are you afraid of giving presentations? Does the very thought of it cause fear? Then this is the book for you! I can't stress enough how exceptional and well thought out this book is. It provides you with all you need to face your next presentation

with confidence, and does so with great attention to detail, yet in an easy-to-follow format."
Claudia L. Meydrech, CN

◆◆◆◆◆

Contents

Acknowledgments

I want to thank my husband for his valuable input and support. Whenever I needed a little assistance with an idea or direction, he was always there to offer his advice. At the mere mention of a need for an image, he began snapping photos until he caught just the right image; including braving the Florida storms to capture the lightening photo used on the cover.

In addition, I would like to thank my good friend, Kim Mutch Emerson, for her editorial guidance. Her talent for seeing the glass half-full instead of half-empty makes it a joy to call her friend.

A special note of thanks to Deepak Morris, Ellen Finkelstein and Dawn Batterbee-Miller, for their willingness to proofread and make suggestions that were both needed and appreciated.

Finally, I want to thank my mother and father for giving me the natural talent and love for words along with a good dose of stage presence.

Introduction

Why a book on presentational skills? Why would I want to author it? The answers to these questions are complex but it all boils down to the dire need for an authoritative source of information that addresses the issues of today's technology.

Much has changed over the years in the public speaking arena. We have so many new and challenging tools at our disposal that we are no longer consigned to countless hours to travel from city to city to share our knowledge.

The Internet has opened the doors to people from all places and races. At the click of a button, you can share your information in many forms of multi-media. With the availability of hosting online conferences and collaborations in both text-only and A/V environments, as are offered by Skype Conference™, Hot Conference™ and desktop sharing applications such as Yugma™, as well as teleconferences, the modes and means are so plentiful that more and more savvy business owners are venturing into the public speaking arena.

It is for you, the farsighted entrepreneur, that this book is written.

What follows is a well thought out, concise, instructional manual written in a manner that all can comprehend. Within the contents of this guide, you will learn the skills necessary to enable you to present your information in such a way that you will capture the attention and hearts of your eager audience.

Whether your goal is to gain the knowledge of putting together a presentation that will enhance your delivery or learn how to conquer your fear of public speaking, you will find the answers here to spur you on to success.

Perhaps your need is to focus on delivery rather than on design. Successfully presenting your information in a manner that will enable you to promote your products or services is presented in the final chapter, The Close. By learning the techniques described in chapter 17, you can stimulate your audience to take the desired action.

The choice is yours, skip to the chapter that you wish to grasp its concepts or read this book from cover to cover. Either way, I am certain that you will gain the knowledge and understanding that will enable you to become the successful public speaker that you envision.

At the very end of this book, you will find a valuable resource section. I have included it in this latest version because you asked for it. It is by no means an exhaustive reference but merely a guide to help you further your knowledge and skill. The resources listed have been reviewed and/or known to me personally as an authoritative source of valuable information and assistance.

Begin your journey by utilizing the tips and techniques you will find here. Then continue building on your knowledge base by practicing the skills you obtain.

Welcome to the world of public speaking,

Ginger Marks

Understanding Your Needs

When was the last time you suffered through a flip board presentation? Was it used in your last corporate conference? I very much doubt it. In today's Internet savvy environment, presentations are no longer limited to the flip chart or chalkboard. More and more individuals and corporations alike are making use of the digital environment to provide efficient and effective communication. Everything from the simple slideshow to live teleconferences, audio/visual productions, and even stand-alone kiosk exhibits are quickly taking over the marketplace.

For this reason, we are seeing presentations become more of a team effort rather than the one-man show of the past. **We expect well presented, visually stimulating presentations.** Software tools that digitally render and manipulate images, video and sound bites that enhance the slides, and the savvy designers who employ their skill to pull it all together, are necessary components of a properly formatted presentational output.

You too can learn these skills. Most powerful and effective slideshows are created with the use of a simple yet powerful software tool called PowerPoint.

As this is the most used design tool, I will focus on this software package in this discussion. Remember though, the  visual part of your workshop or seminar is merely the starting point. Unless you have mastered your oral presentation and your handouts support your dialogue you may do more harm than good. We will touch briefly on all of these issues as this discussion progresses.

There are basically two reasons to give a presentation. The first is to *offer information* and the second to *offer an idea or opinion* that may not be widely known or accepted. What type of information you are attempting to provide, and who your audience is, should be of primary importance at this juncture. Are you trying to inform a group of corporate types that what your company has to offer will affect their bottom line and is therefore the best tool available for the challenge they are facing, or are you simply reviewing the year-end corporate production ratios? As you can see, there is a good reason to utilize both methods.

Regardless of the form you choose, whether informative or persuasive, stick with the theme throughout your entire staging. Switching in midstream from one to the other, or jumping back and forth, may further confuse your audience instead of clarifying your point of view.

As is true with all speeches, who you are speaking to, and your final desired outcome, will help you determine which type of presentation you will want to give.

Know your goal

You know your goal is to ensure that the information you relate will be easily understood and accepted. Keep in mind that people, overall, are easily confused and confounded. The last thing you want to do is to be the source of that confusion.

Decide which type of information you need to offer to affect your desired result, before beginning the design process. This will help you stay on track.

Consider the main point you want to make and carefully guide your discussion down the path to its action-stimulating conclusion. This *theme* is the main *takeaway* that you want your audience to accept. If you can, *boil this down into one key sentence.* You will refer back to this thought as your presentation develops.

Let me show you how to do this. We will call our company *Kookware.* Don't laugh; I imagine silly looking cookware would flood the market if it were invented.

We begin our fictitious presentation by stating our desired goal. In this case, our end result will be to show the superiority of our cookware company's products. Therefore, we know quite easily that the desired result is to persuade. In the process of persuasion you will be offering information, this is true. However, offering information will be the tool we use and not the theme of our presentation. To uncover the theme we need to dig a bit deeper.

Let's start with a few true statements about our company. Kookware is the new generation of cookware. It entices the younger generation to get back into the kitchen. It does this by making cooking fun and funky. In the process of creating home cooked meals, they will eat healthier and save money over fast food dining.

All of these statements are true about Kookware, but we only need one *takeaway* statement to be able to proceed. Consider which one to use, if any, by looking at it from your audiences' perspective. What you need to prove to them is the *benefit* not the feature. Look at the previous statements and find the one that will be the most helpful in convincing your audience that owning your product is not only a wise purchasing decision but also a reasonable motivation for them to take action at the close of your presentation. After all, your goal is to motivate them to purchase your Kookware.

In looking at the previous list, the one that stands out is the final statement. "In the process of creating home cooked meals, they will eat healthier and save money over fast food dining." This seems a bit wordy and long so let's boil this down into one concise thought. Our *key sentence* develops into an easy to remember statement. **Using Kookware can save you money and promote long life.**

You see how easy that was. Taking the time to work through this process will keep you on the path to presenting a successful and purposeful presentation. One that will spur your audience to take the action steps necessary to take advantage of your offering.

Who's Listening

Why should you care? You have one message to share that everyone listening wants to hear, or they wouldn't be in your audience. However, whom you are speaking to will definitely affect how you share your speech and the support medium(s) you choose.

When speaking to a group of professionals you will want to use a voice of authority and conviction. Present a respectful and peer-to-peer stance. On the other hand, when speaking to a group of newly hired employees your demeanor and tone should be more commanding and assertive. You may have the same message to get across, but you simply need to tailor it to fit your audience.

What you say is important. Of equal significance, is to whom you have to say it. Unless and until you know whom you will be speaking to, you will not be able to prepare your presentation in any meaningful manner. There are several specifics that you should be aware of prior to writing the very first word. Some of the clearly identifiable, significant aspects that you should consider include:

- Age
- Gender
- Size
- Location
- Education
- Entrance requirements
- Technology level

The *age, gender,* and *education* of your audience are easily defined. You may need to query your host/hostess to help you determine these and other aspects. As to *size,* I am simply implying that you may consider a much more compact version of your presentation when addressing a small audience. But, whereas with a larger assembly, you may want to be a bit more specific in your facts and figures.

Is your presentation aimed at a group of medical professionals? Does it center on the latest advances in telomerase based anti-cancer therapy, or are you speaking to a group of schoolchildren? Obviously, the information you would present on this topic would vary greatly depending on this important aspect.

Location too is an important consideration. The size and layout of the room are not the only items of interest when planning your delivery. We will discuss this in more depth later.

Entrance requirements, as well, will have an impact on your presentation. Though, perhaps one of the least significant factors, it should still be considered. When your audience is attending a free seminar, they may be a bit more forgiving. On the other hand, when you find yourself in front of a paying audience they will expect a more correct and professional staging.

Many business owners have come to realize that giving their information without compensation is the easiest and most lucrative way to get in front of a qualified audience.

Why give away your information? Why share your knowledge for free? The answer is summed up in one word, opportunity. Many groups, clubs, and organizations need speakers for their events, but do not have a specific budget set aside to compensate a speaker.

When you agree to speak in front of a group for free, you will find them both appreciative and accepting. Since there are more of these situations available, the possibility of connecting with someone who will be interested in your product or service is much greater.

Another benefit is the opportunity to test your speech. As I mentioned earlier, in the small group, pro-bono, setting your audience is much more forgiving. Therefore, this is the perfect circumstance for you to try out your workshop or seminar on an audience to see where you need to tweak it.

If you want to take advantage of this opportunity I suggest you check with both online and offline sources. Civic clubs and Chambers are always looking for speakers. While working as a Financial Advisor I found speaking to the local senior citizen organization on a monthly basis to be most beneficial. I simply approached them with the idea of scheduling speakers for their members and they jumped at the idea. In this way, I was able to promote others and occasionally present my information while at the same time, as the person in charge of scheduling, I was considered by all an authoritative figure.

Finding online sources to speak is just as easy. To begin with, use a search engine to locate Podcasts and networks that host regular programs whose audience is your 'target' market. The owners of those resources are always delighted to find a speaker who fits their niche and will bring value to their listeners and members.

The opportunities are out there if you are willing to spend time searching for them.

As for *technology level*, this is simply how tech-savvy they are. Are they used to the bells and whistles or would an all-out tech heavy presentation leave them confused and unimpressed. Save the time and effort of presenting a tech-heavy  presentation for the audience that would better appreciate it. On the other side of this coin you may find that the tech-savvy audience may not have the attention span to read all the handouts and such that are part of the more traditional presentation.

For smaller audiences or one-on-ones you may find that a simple flip chart, white board, and/or handouts are all that is needed to give an effective presentation. Remember you are not there to wow your audience, rather to present an idea and the facts to substantiate it.

For the more tech-savvy audience items that you may consider employing—to enhance your slide presentation—could include tools like a laser pointer, a lapel or head set microphone, transparencies, films, computer projections as well as your slides. Oh, and let us not forget the ever faithful overhead projector.

When employing any technical utilities, like the laser pointer, microphone, projection equipment and the like, always test it out prior to the event. One of the most embarrassing moments you could ever have is beginning your presentation only to find out that your equipment is not functioning as planned. Not only is this embarrassing, making a nervous presenter even more on edge, but it can also leave your audience questioning your expertise.

In the area of presentational software, of the available programs on the market today, PowerPoint has been, and still is, the forerunner. It is a simple to use software package.

PowerPoint has pre-designed slide templates that make the task of creating an eye appealing presentation a simple undertaking. We will discuss this program and some of its capabilities a little later in this book. You will find this discussion in the chapter titled, Creating Your Slideshow.

Briefly, PowerPoint provides the ability to include not only sophisticated graphs and complex charts but small bits of audio and video can now be embedded in your slideshow. As with any audio byte be sure to limit its use, as many people still find unexpected audio bites not only distracting but also annoying. These are best used for stand-alone kiosk presentations where the job is to capture the passerby's attention long enough to get your message across. In this instance, the audio and video can kick your slides up just enough to accomplish your goal.

Handouts are a must have for most presentations. Audiences of all ages like to have something to hold on to. Not only does it allow them a place to write down their thoughts, but it further allows you to include points that you might want to include but would clutter your slide presentation.

Handouts can be in the form of copies of your slides with space for note taking or they can be copies of materials that further enhance or lend credibility to your subject matter. For an example, if you wanted to refer to a credible source but don't want to cover the material in its entirety during your presentation you might refer to the handout and make your audience aware of further information found in it about the subject matter.

With the availability of 'Safe disk' technology you may find it less expensive to burn your handout materials such as brochures, flyers, business materials, upcoming schedule, evaluation sheet, etc. to a CD or DVD rather than printing, compiling, and providing them in hard copy form. This is an option that you may want to provide at the end of your seminar as a means of building your mailing list. I will discuss this in further detail later on.

Whatever your presentation objective might be, the key is to practice. If you fail to practice your presentation until you are comfortable with what you want to say and how you want to say it, at minimum, you will leave your audience unimpressed.

I highly recommend that if you plan to introduce physical objects you should work with those as well. You may find that the handling of an object you thought would enhance your point just doesn't 'feel right' when you are going through your practice session. It is much wiser to realize and adjust prior to your event rather than experiencing those discoveries during your presentation.

Beginning the Design

Now you can let the artist in you loose. Let your imagination soar. Write down everything that comes to mind. You will hone this list as your outline develops.

So how do you begin? What is an outline? Your outline contains those *key points* you want to make and *supporting evidence* to back them up. This evidence will be provided as charts and graphs, physical objects, or real-life stories. Whatever you use, be certain that it elaborates on your point and clarifies your position. Anything from facts and figures to statements from authority figures are viable tools for use in your presentations.

An authority figure is a broad concept. The best authority to quote is one with which your audience is familiar. For example, when speaking to a group of children you might quote a famous actor that they all know, like Barney. However, if your audience is older your choice might come from a noted author or even a person in politics. The point here is to use a person of note to the audience you are speaking. To quote someone that they may not know can still work for you, but if the authority figure is someone that the audience can relate to then the information will more readily be accepted as fact.

You may even find it useful to simply provide a definition of a word. Be sure that your definition is a direct quote from a leading dictionary or encyclopedia and not just your own interpretation.

Years ago, this limited us to sources like Encyclopedia Britannica, Merriam-Webster, and Random House College Dictionary. Today you will find a whole host of resources available to you.

Some of the most frequently referenced online sources include but are not limited to

Bartleby
Wikipedia
Urban Dictionary

Another idea is to search quote listings online. Some of the sources I find helpful are

Woopidoo
Quotations Page
Leadership Now
The Quote Garden

You will find numerous subject headings to investigate from politicians to authors. Consider also the international, multi-cultural language quotes. Sometimes a quote stated in a foreign language can add a little pizzazz to an otherwise boring quote. You will find translation software quite helpful here. There is one word of warning however; online versions of translation software are choppy translations at best. If you have decided to use this tool, you may find it worth the cost to pay a service to translate the quote for you. This will lend credibility to your foreign quote. Be sure you know the proper pronunciation of the words. Not only will this make you more comfortable at the time of rendering the quote but any members of the audience who just happen to speak that language will not cringe and then discount or miss the whole rest of your presentation. Combining evidence can lend to both an effective argument and keep your listeners attention.

The most valuable tools to use are jokes and real-life stories. Whether humorous or heartfelt you will find that these tools will help break up the monotony of your presentation. You will find more on this subject later in this book. Go to the chapter on The Presentation to learn more.

Organize your thoughts so that they flow. The best presentations flow easily from one topic to the next. Try to stay on the path and guide your audience with clearly defined steps. Don't just haphazardly jump from point to point. Ordering your thoughts can be accomplished several ways. Try to choose the one that best fits your need. Among the options available to you are:

Topical
- The discussion of a specific topic of importance
- Lends to analysis and proof presentation
- Often followed by Q&A

Chronological
- The presentation of a series of events
- Lends well to artistic presentations where the artist's works are followed from birth to death
- Lends well to product development presentations

Classification
- Also known as categorical
- Can show relative value
- Utilized to offer principles of significant difference
- Provides a basis for clarification of issues

Problem/Solution

- Present a problem and develop a logical solution
- Quotable sources
- Requires a clearly defined transition between the problem and the solution
- Explain how the solution affects different parts of the problem or of the whole, as applicable

Cause/Effect

- Present root cause and end result of a situation
- Offer the remedy
- Requires clearly defined transition between cause and effect
- Lends well to environmental and governmental issues

As you can see each of these methods have their purpose. One is not better than the other for every seminar or workshop you do. **Every presentation you give will have different needs.** Pick one method and stick with it. Mixing these paths

will only lead to confusion causing your audience to lose track of the point you are trying to make. Use one, and only one, method and transition from topic to topic smoothly so that your message will have a balanced flow. We will discuss transitions in more detail in the next chapter.

Transitioning

Transitioning throughout your presentations is the tool you will use to smoothly move from one thought to the next. What you say or do not say to carry the audience from one point to the next can either effectively keep your audience with you or have them floundering for a connection. Go back to the end of the previous chapter in this book and re-read that last paragraph. Do you see how effectively I helped you realize that the previous subject was concluded and we were moving on to the next? Without effective transitions your audience will 'catch up', however while they are trying to make the connection themselves, they won't be listening and will probably miss some of your presentation.

> Without effective transitions, your audience will be busy playing catch-up.

There are **three typical ways to transition** between your points; the first is *review*, the second is to *remind* and the third is to *inform*.

Review is used to reinforce earlier points and help them understand where you are heading. It also is a clear demarcation that you have finished your previous point. One easy way to achieve this with the use of review is to begin your transition with a statement such as, "We have discussed..."

Remind, on the other hand, can be used to demonstrate to your audience how your points have led up to where you are now. This transition type solidifies in their minds the key points you want them to remember. Simply repeat your key point. You might begin this transitional statement with, "Don't forget..." or "We discovered earlier..."

While both review and remind are the best ways to transition your audience from one focal point to the next the third is probably the most common, Inform.

To **inform** your audience where you are headed next and what your focus is changing to, simply stated, clearly demonstrates that the previous topic is concluded and that there is more information that you have prepared to share.

As you have already surmised, this is the transitional tool I used at the conclusion of the last chapter.

All of these transition types can be used in your presentation interchangeably. In fact, the best presentations do just that. As mentioned earlier, practice until you are comfortable. Missing even one transition due to timing or nervousness can be costly to your overall message.

Remember, your audience wasn't there beside you moment by moment as you pondered what you were going to share, whittled down to your key statement, sat beside you as you doggedly prepared your presentation, or was privy to those 'in front of the mirror' hours of practice that the days leading up to your live presentation entailed.

Keep them aware and informed and help them see where you have been and where you are going.

Miss even one transition and you risk losing them.

Visuals

Visuals aids spice up your presentation when used properly. They are often used as transitional elements. However, they are **most effective when used to clarify your points.** Visual aids successfully turn your words into pictures.

Regardless of your audience, it is a well-known fact that the best presentations provide visual as well as aural stimulation. How often have you heard it said that to increase your retention you should use all the tools available to you: sight, sound, touch, smell, and taste? It is further proven, to increase retention, you need to use at least three of the above senses within your presentation.

As an example, you will find that giving your audience visual stimulation and a place to write their thoughts down will increase retention significantly over merely speaking to them.

Your visual aids should
- Improve your audience's understanding of the topic
- Supply variety to your presentation

- Support your claims
- Reinforce your points
- Generate more impact to help listeners remember your presentation

These aids do not need to all be presented on a slide. You may find that the use of a physical object such as a book or yardstick could be just as effective.

Think about which points and evidence you want to get across and which presentation aids will help you communicate them. After you have narrowed down your selections, consider if they are right for the room in which you will be speaking and, most of all, the audience you will be addressing.

I still remember a chamber networking event that I attended, a few years ago. When it came time for a fellow Financial Advisor to give his five-minute introduction, he offered a quick presentation on retirement.

The reason his presentation stays with me is that he utilized a wooden yardstick. As he talked about the way we think at different ages about saving for retirement he broke off a section of the yardstick.

Imagine the impact that had on others in the room who were not 'in the business' if it made that much of an impact on me. Make sure your visuals are impactful and you too will be remembered long after your presentation has ended.

Things to consider when selecting visuals are the audience's comprehension of your subject matter; would a visual aid assist the understanding of your point or just fill in where you could talk them through? Would your key points be better shown by example? Are your visual aids practical? Will you be able to locate, transport and manipulate them without great difficulty? If the answer is no, then let that idea go and find something a bit easier to obtain and handle.

Imagine that you are speaking to a group of car manufacturers about a new concept you have for their latest model. Sure, it would be spectacular for you to bring to the platform your special hybrid model, but it might not be practical or advisable, let alone easy to obtain. A much better solution to your visual aid might be photographs of the buying public that your concept car will attract.

Does your model save them money at the pump? Bring a toy pump and smash it. That would be something they would remember later and then maybe they would remember you too. If nothing else, it will break up the monotony.

How much time you have for your presentation can also determine not only how many visuals to use but if you should incorporate them at all. Consider what equipment you will have available as well as the layout of the room. When preparing a presentation for the senior community center you may not need to spend time creating a flashy, technically advanced presentation. Handouts and giveaways may be your best choice.

A senior adult audience would probably be satisfied with a quick, inexpensive black & white printed copy of your presentational slides with room to write comments. For them

you can put these in a nice folder or just staple them together. Either hand them out at the door or place them at each seat with a pencil or pen for note taking.

However, when presenting to a technically savvy audience they have come to expect the flash and have little or no need for handouts. If you do include handouts for this audience, you may want to present them after the close of your presentation in the form of a well-designed informational packet.

If it is appropriate, invest in personalized pens. These are inexpensive and well accepted. If lost or given away, your business information is passed along to the new owner. Suffice it to say, your business card is better on a pen than on paper.

For a small group the use of simple tools may be more effective. Flip charts, white boards, overheads and handouts can skillfully stimulate audience participation. On the flipside, these types of tools can be difficult to transport. For example, my vehicle is a Mazda Miata. While it is both economical and fun to drive, if you are familiar with that car you know that not much will fit into one. It barely fits the week's groceries for two. Obviously, it would never accommodate a flip chart. Therefore, when I need a flipchart I found that the local office store carries

a nice foldable presentation folder. This sits neatly on the table or dais in front of me and I can make notes on the backs of each insert for stimulation, in case I need it.

No matter what you choose or how advanced your audience, consideration should be given to the handouts. While the smaller, less technically savvy audience would be comfortable with a digitally printed, stapled handout, you want to be sure the opposite group is presented with a handout that is printed on a color laser printer and presented in a compact form such as a binder or folder. Even better for this audience is the CD or DVD.

Handouts effectively

- Give your audience a handy reference for use throughout a presentation.
- Gives your audience a catch-up point if they get lost
- Spares your listeners excessive note-taking
- Enables you to include information that you may not have time to present
- Ensures your audience will take your message home with them

Passing physical objects around the room, while presenting, is another effective use of visual aids. As you probably already know, touch, in and of itself, is used to solidify your points. Our senses should be stimulated in order to ensure your message is indelibly imprinted on your audience. If your presentation does not lend itself to an easily handled object (e.g., an automobile or airplane), as stated earlier, you might consider photographs of the object as a viable alternative.

Now that we have considered the non-technical presentational tools, I would like to change our focus to the technical side of things. Digital tools have enabled presenters to quickly and easily incorporate many aspects into our presentations that would have been difficult, at best, to present prior to the digital age.

With the use of software, a laptop computer, and computer projection equipment, you can easily include not just a digital slideshow but multi-media objects. You can create a visually stimulating presentation that incorporates charts & graphs, images, text, audio and even video with the technology available today. Not only can you create your presentation digitally, you can download it to a CD or DVD for ease of transportation. With the use of the newest 'Safe Disk' technology, you can even ensure that your presentation stays on the CD or DVD and doesn't add hidden files to the host computer. With the plethora of viruses and such this is of foremost concern to your viewers as well as your host.

The only drawback to digital presentations is in the setup. If you are not sure of the connections or how to set up your equipment prior to show time be sure you have someone with you who can help with this process. Also, there is the chance that something might go awry during your presentation, God forbid. Having a technically knowledgeable assistant can make all the difference in getting you back on track. In the event that the situation is not correctable, for example, the light in the projector blows and you don't have a replacement handy, you may want to have a backup plan in place. This is where your handouts can come in mighty handy.

If your presentation is to be given to a large audience in a big room, you will definitely want to use a voice amplification system of one sort or another. A hands-free microphone such as a headset or lapel microphone not only allows you to be heard but also frees your hands for handling your props, the slide changer, or perhaps even a digital laser pointer.

Organizing

Now it is time to begin compiling your materials and preparing for your event. Knowing the venue and the expected audience's size and details will assist you in providing an effective, efficient presentation.

Online presentations can now encompass both audio and visual as well as chat capabilities. These venues are often easier to work with as they are limited only by the server. If you find that, your server is not capable of handling the expected numbers of attendees you will want to increase your bandwidth before the event.

However, when your venue is live there are several factors you should take into consideration. Size is an important factor. If your room is larger than your audience, you may have trouble keeping their attention. One way to combat this problem is to ask them to localize in the room. This seems to be the solution for the last minute low turnout and provides an intimate one-on-one ambiance for the attendees.

When the opposite is true, be prepared to provide extra seating or at least, standing or floor space. No matter what the size, be sure the chairs are spaced so that your audience has a comfortable view of the presentation area.

As mentioned earlier, test your electrical hookups and equipment to ensure they are in proper working order. Make absolutely certain that you are familiar with the Audio/Visual (AV) tools you will be utilizing. Even when presenting at a familiar venue unexpected challenges can arise.

For example, on one occasion I arrived only to find the air condition was not functioning properly. The solution was to simply, take more breaks to allow for a slight relief even if it was just a chance to get up and move around. This allowed me to keep the audience focused and refreshed. Yes, it did extend the length of the presentation, but that was much preferred to having a distracted audience and ineffective delivery of my message.

Speaking of delivery of your message one of the most frequent mistakes is cramming the slides so full with text that the audience spends more time reading than paying attention to what is relayed. I highly recommend limiting your text to no more than 30% of your slide and enlarging it to provide ease of reading and comprehension. Your audience should not have to spend more than 5 to 10 seconds grasping the link between your visual object and the message you are sharing. You may find that images or physical objects will clarify your point more quickly than text.

Keep the size of your text and graphics on the large side. This will make it easier for those sitting farthest from your presentation to see and read them. Remember, you should consider your room and audience sizes when choosing just how much to enlarge these visual objects.

While oversized text and graphics are a requirement for visual clarity in a large group setting, close-up, one-on-one, over-the-table presentations, such as I gave more often than not, when sharing about financial planning, the size of these objects was usually somewhat smaller.

This doesn't give you a free license to cram your slides with elements. Remember, you want them to listen to what you have to say. The key is clarity. Your slides, no matter what size audience, are simply a tool to provide clarity to what you are sharing.

When your viewer is reading the slide, they are obviously too busy to grasp what you are saying. They may hear you, but not HEAR you.

One way to combat this problem, other than not providing slides at all, is to give them a moment to view the slide. However, if your slide contains a graph or chart they may need a second longer to fully grasp the content. Asking them if they have any questions, about the particular graphic or slide might be a viable solution.

Clip art has its place, but when you want to provide a professional image steer clear of it. Overused clip art loses its effectiveness and may detract from your presentation. If you can't afford to invest in expensive, original, artwork there are several places you can purchase images for as little as $1 to $5 for use. Some of my favorite sources are listed in the Reference Section of this book.

Be sure to read the copyright information attached to the photos you select. Usually when your usage of the image is restricted to personal use (you are not reselling it), the low cost image copyright license is all you will need to acquire.

Color and contrast are another important consideration when designing your visuals. Keep the colors to a minimum and the contrast at a visually appealing level. There are color wheels available on the web that can assist you in your choices. Another good source is your local paint store. Choose no more than five complimentary colors for your presentation; three would be better. You can always use gradient shades of the same color for variation. To add interest use contrasting colors.

It has been proven, through studies, that humans are attracted to bright colors.

Interestingly, we are not the only ones that are affected by color. A fact I recently learned is that hummingbirds are attracted by bright colors, not scent. In nature and in art color variations are of primary importance to successfully establish a thought or desired end result.

Consider the stop sign. It is a bright red as this is a power color, commanding attention. Be careful not to overplay this card; too bright and you run the risk of not only offending your viewers, but actually hurting their eyes. There is a reason they call the *red tie* the **power tie**. They don't call it the red suit! If you are still having trouble deciding if your color scheme is well thought out, consider asking a trusted friend or family member their opinion.

One common misconception is that while black text on a white background is widely accepted and actually easiest to read, white text on black is just as acceptable. This is not true, white text on black is neither visually appealing nor easily readable.

I have been informed by clients, who have requested their webpage and/or presentational materials to be created with white on black, that their most common complaint is that it is unreadable or hard to read, at the very least. You will find many dark color backgrounds that are equally offensive with the lighter text. For this reason most of my design work, whether print or digital, internet or book layout, is usually created using a light background with darker text.

Another notion that I have heard is that the easiest to read is yellow text on black. While this may be acceptable for the younger audience, older audiences will disagree. Again, your audience should be taken into consideration when your color choices are made.

In regards to fonts, when creating your presentation, be sure you choose a font style and size that is easy to read from a distance as well as close up. San Serif is the font style of choice for most presentations. San, meaning without, should be easy for you to remember. These non-formal fonts are without added frills or tails. Studies have shown that people can read sans serif better and faster in digital form vs. serif, as opposed to print where the opposite tends to be true. Ninety-nine percent of all websites utilize san serif fonts; take my advice and follow their lead.

Consistency is paramount; utilize one or two fonts, no more. For titles, I consistently select a font size between 36-48 points. The body of your slides should remain constant in the range of 26 to 32 points. I am not saying to vary your font sizes within this scale on each slide, rather choose a point size within this range and consistently utilize it on all of your slides. If you set these specifications in your master slide you won't have to worry about whether your slides stay consistent. Also, if you set up your master slide rather than using a blank slide for each new slide and drawing out your text boxes on them you will ensure that the layout of the text on the slide won't jump around from slide to slide as you transition through your presentation.

Verdana is a San Serif font that is slightly less used than Arial.

BondiMT and Times New Roman are good examples of Serif fonts.

Every designer knows the importance of properly proportioned white space. So, don't crowd your slides. Less is more! Remember the 5 to 10 second rule.

Be sure to use capitalization properly. Only capitalize the first letter of a sentence and proper nouns. Anything more than that is not only annoying but tends to offend those who know better. For readability, you may want to adhere to left justified text rather than fully justified.

While justified text is perfect for a book or report. On your slides the extra space that is added in order to justify the content is blown out of proportion. What may look good on your screen, when projected through a projector onto a big screen will look strangely spaced. Again, consider your audience. You don't want them distracted by the slide but rather attracted to what you have to share. Eliminate anything that might hamper your audience's attention and retention. Even a minor point like justification can and will make a big difference.

Bulleted text, charts, graphs, and images should not overpower the layout or be over used. Keep these elements to a level where they are incorporated into your presentation, not your presentation integrated into them.

You may not use graphs and charts as often as you do graphics and bullet list items. Nevertheless, for the appropriate audience they may be your best alternative.

One idea that seems to work better than the simple bullet point is a nice graphic element in place of the bullet. Try this idea and see how it works. You need no longer suffer the boring bullet pointed text.

Be sure to review your presentation, not only for misspellings and proper grammar, but factual data as well. You want to be ready to answer any questions about the data you are presenting in a confident manner. If you are not sure of your facts your audience will pick that up and your credibility will be damaged beyond repair. Don't wait until your facts are questioned to find you only know the fact and not the supporting data. Footnotes are excellent places to put this information for handy reference. And they can be easily added to your handouts. When you add the resources list to the handouts if questioned you can refer your audience to the handout. That way, if you forget the source, you have it there to reference too.

For most of my small group sessions, I prefer to provide a copy of my slides and a space to write notes in my handouts. Therefore, the amount of information I provide in them gives them just enough to follow along with me and is provided at the beginning of the presentation.

If you are going to provide an information packet consider handing it out after your presentation. Either way, be sure to include your business card or at least your contact information in each packet. This should include your name, business name, address, phone numbers, website and email addresses minimally. If you have a blog address or additional information that is relative, you should consider including that as well. However, don't get carried away and add all your contact sources. For example, if you give them your Facebook and Skype IDs are you really ready for all the people that will contact you through those sources? If the answer is yes, then by all means add it. If not, then don't.

To provide the polished look of a properly planned handout always print them on a laser printer as opposed to an inkjet. The quality is immediately apparent. If you are presenting to your audience in an informal setting you might get away with just the sheets stapled together. However, when you want to put your best foot forward I highly recommend you incorporate color laser prints, bind them with a binding such as Velo, Spiral, or Comb, and insert that into a folder that has a cutout for your business card to fit neatly into. If your packet is over twenty pages, you may want to consider including tab indexes to make it easier for your attendees to locate specific items in your package. Tabs also make it easier for you to instruct them how to find a page you are referencing when you want them to follow along.

Embedded Objects

The good news is charts and graphs are easily inserted into PowerPoint slides. After creating your chart or graph in one of the available software applications, such as Excel, importing them into your presentation is as easy as inserting an image. The commands to complete this task are pretty straight forward. Depending on what version you use, it could be as simple as: **Insert > Chart Options, select Chart Category and Chart Type within the Category**, click **OK** to insert the chart.

In PowerPoint 2007, to import your chart data, **select the active chart. Activate the Chart Tools Design** tab and click **Edit Data**. Inside Excel, for example, select the **Data** tab and click the **Options** in the **Get External Data** group. What could be simpler?

It is always wise to describe in your heading what your chart or graph is reflecting rather than just naming it something generic.

This helps the audience immediately understand the purpose for the graph.

Use the proper graph style to represent the information you are presenting.

Line graphs are used to graph one or more dependent variables, on the vertical axis, as functions of an independent variable on the horizontal axis. Example: a graph of a person's height and weight (two dependent variables) as a function of age (the independent variable).

A pie chart, on the other hand, may be more appropriate for com-paring given objects at a point in time. Example: an investor's portfolio on a given date e.g., 5% Money Market, 10% CDs and 85% Stocks.

For further information, I would recommend Reinhard Diestel's excellent *Introduction to Graph Theory*. You will find the link in the resource section.

Video and audio files are just as simple to embed in a PowerPoint slide. These types of files can be created in a number of ways. With today's technology, you no longer are a slave to the video editing professional. Be warned though, if quality and time are issues and you don't have the knowledge base to create a professional A/V you may be better off hiring someone who can assist you. There are Virtual Assistants (VAs) that specialize in this area at a fraction of the cost of your local TV station. Yes, as funny as this may sound, there is such a thing as an A/V VA!

If you don't have any idea how to locate a reputable A/V VA I am certain that my A/V VA would be happy to assist you with your project. The company I consistently hire for just this sort of specialty work is listed on the resource pages.

Keeping in mind the additional cost of development and time to create them you may want to use this additional tool when you know you will be able to make the best use of it. My opinion is that video is best for big crowds in a big room and for presentations that you will utilize again and again.

Creating your Slideshow

If I may offer a word of warning, I would suggest that you **beware of the bells and whistles**. Be careful that you do not overuse the transitional slide elements. Keep it simple and professional. **Make yourself the star and not your presentation.** PowerPoint offers a variety of pre-manufactured templates. They come in a variety of colors and textures.

To begin creating your slides, select a template. In selecting the proper template, there are a couple of things to keep in mind. Who your audience is will also influence your choice of template. What I mean by this is that in a corporate setting a simple background is the preferred template. A design that will not interfere with the presentation itself is best. In the corporate setting, I recommend using either a solid color background in conservative colors such as black, brown, green, or blue. For a touch of interest, you may want to use a gradient or a lightly textured background. These types of templates are readily found or easily created and should be considered for use if you are presenting to a large audience. Simple single color, slight gradient or lightly textured templates allow the text to be clearly read from a much farther distance.

In a smaller group you can use a more expressive background. A computer kiosk used by a single viewer or an online A/V chat room environment as well as a small classroom work well for these templates. Remember to keep the text to a minimum on both these types of templates to allow your audience to instantly read and absorb the content so that the focus remains on what you are saying instead of the content of the slide.

To select a design template or to build your own design in PowerPoint 2007, click the **Design Tab**. *Note: In previous versions of PowerPoint the term used is 'template'*. For all intents and purposes, the template of old has been reclassified in 2007 to 'theme'. This allows the theme to be available cross-platform for uniformity of Microsoft Office Suite® programs. So where did the template go? Templates still exist; the difference is they can now contain content.

While the new themes provide both beauty and functionality in color and design, the layout is meant to provide you with a consistent slide positioning of elements. These layouts are classified by type in the familiar styles of *Title Slide, Title and Content, Section Header, Two Content, Comparison, Title Only, Blank, Content and Caption, and Picture with Caption.*

In the *Design Tab* **select** from the available **themes** or browse for more themes by selecting the down arrow to the lower right of the available theme window. To choose the theme, all you need to do is click. Once that selection is made, you can easily alter the colors to better fit your preference. To make these adjustments the first step is to click **Colors** in the pane just to the right of the themes. Then click the **Create New Theme Colors** link at the bottom of the drop down box that appears.

Next, in the *Create New Theme Colors* dialogue box select an area in which to change the theme color, such as Accent 1, click the arrow next to the color shown and a color chart will appear. From there you can**, select a new color**, and then **Rename** and **Save** to apply. *Note: Always name your new color scheme for the obvious reasons*. At this point, you will see your new color scheme applied to the slide. Making these changes in your *Slide Master* will enable you to quickly modify the entire presentation.

If you don't see a theme that fits quite what you are looking for, even with color modification, you might find the professionally designed templates and backgrounds in **PowerFinish,** available through www.PowerFinish.com, appropriate for your needs. Not only are these designs clean and professional but they are provided as a download. I have used these templates and backgrounds myself when designing for clients. Be aware that personal use is without additional requirement. However, to utilize these designs from PowerFinish for professional resale use, you will need to purchase the additional developer rights, as I did. I am sure there are other resources for template design, but these are my preference when I don't have the time to design them myself.

Like me, if you have design talent you may want to design your theme yourself. However, if you don't have design experience stick with the themes that are provided or purchasable, period. That being said, to begin your design you will want to create a background for both the title and the content slides. They should be sized to fit your presentation needs. The standard slide is 1024- by 768-pixels.

Once you have decided on the theme and templates you will use to pull your presentation together, it is time to consider the images you will employ. We spoke briefly about images in Chapter 6. If you need to refresh your memory, go back and read it again now.

The images you use should either enliven or enhance your presentation. At the risk of repeating myself, remember that your slide show is an extension of your presentation and not the other way around.

One of the techniques that I find most beneficial is to include an image of something that powerfully illustrates one key point in an amusing manner.

As an example, when pulling together a presentation for a monthly club meeting for a client, one key point he wanted to make was the types of people who use the internet. He wanted to stress that there is something to be found there for everyone. I suggested he find a photo that would both amuse and enhance rather than just using text. His choice was of a kitten wearing a grapefruit peal helmet. Yes, a real hollowed out grapefruit! You can just about image the reaction of the audience. Not only did he report back that they got a giggle, but they paid closer attention to the rest of the presentation.

However cute his choice was, it failed the relevancy check. It was not just slightly, but way off-topic and research shows that irrelevant images reduce memory of the content. Yes, they'll remember the slide, and him, but will they remember the content?

Use transitions wisely. Too many transitions between slides and your audience will be oohing and awing at the presentation and not listening to what you have to say.

There are a number of different transitions available in PowerPoint. You will find these in the handy **Animations** tab. The transitions you will find there include the more familiar *Blinds, Checkerboard, Fade Smoothly, Fade Through Black, Cut, Cut Through Black, Dissolve, Zoom, Split & Wipe,* along with some new ones like *Wheel and Push.* All of these options give you additional choices of direction. One of my favorites to use that really lets your audience know something important is on the way is the *Newsflash* transition.

In the old days if you wanted to create a *Fade from black* on your first slide you had to create one black slide and transition from that into your presentation. Likewise, you had to do the same at the end of your presentation. In PowerPoint 2007™, you now have the *Fade through Black* and *Cut through Black* available on any and all of your slides at the click of your mouse.

Note that if timing is a concern you may find the quicker Wipe is what you are looking for rather than the slower Fade transition.

So much more could be said about presentation design and development. However, since there are numerous books on that subject and this book is meant as a guide for giving your presentation rather than creating the physical slides so I won't go into a lot of the nuances and instructions here.

One such source that I highly recommend for a new designer is the *Cutting Edge PowerPoint 2007* by Geetesh Bajaj from the For Dummies series. This and many other items of interest can be found in the Resource Section in the back of this book.

One of the newest, most useful features in PowerPoint 2010 is the ability to embed video files straight from off YouTube. Just copy and paste the code from YouTube anywhere into any slide, and whallah, your video is embedded into your presentation!

Do you love to fiddle with the video frames? Guess what? In 2010 you have been given the chance. Yes, video editing right within the new PowerPoint 2010. I could go on and on, because this is just the tip of the proverbial iceberg. If you are into all the techo-gizmo stuff, you will love the new PowerPoint.

If you are not a novice at presentation design with PowerPoint and are looking for something that will enable you to add polish to your slides check out another of Geetesh's latest releases titled, *PowerPoint 2007 Complete Makeover Kit.* This book was a joint effort by Geetesh and Echo Swinford.

Are you a visual learner? Do you want to know everything about the new PowerPoint 2010? Check out the book *Teach Yourself VISUALLY PowerPoint 2010* by William Wood, Bill Wood.

Pack and Go

When you are packing the car to head to your appointment there are several things that you should take along besides your presentation itself.

These items include any AV equipment you might need, projector, laptop, backups of any digital files and images on CDs, DVDs, or flash drives, visual aids and copies of your visual aids, including photo copies, extra slides, handouts and perhaps, a spare flip chart.

It is also a good idea to take along spare batteries for all your equipment, including for your laptop, an extension cord, and a few three-prong to two-prong adaptors, A/V cables and adaptors for them to assure you can hook up to any TV, speaker, or other equipment. Don't forget your business cards, markers, pens and pencils, note cards and backup note cards.

You may want to number your note cards just in case they get tossed about, or worse, dropped during your presentation. This is a definite possibility and the confusion and nerves take over when that happens. To avoid these uncomfortable moments **number your note cards ahead of time**. Realize that if you do drop them it is OK to laugh and joke with your audience to relieve the tension and ask the audience for a brief moment while you put them back in order.

Bottles of water and a change of clothes would also probably be a good idea if you have room. I will get into proper attire in the next chapter aptly titled, Dress for Success. For now, suffice it to say dress comfortably yet err on the side of conservativeness.

Now that you have your basic tools organized and accounted for, you need to pack your presentation itself. With PowerPoint 2007 utilizing the **Pack and Go** PowerPoint feature to transfer your presentation to CD or DVD allows not only the presentation but the fonts and graphic objects to be embedded on the transfer device. The benefit of this is that if for any reason you have to use a secondary computer to host your presentation you will have all of the necessary parts in one place to successfully display it.

> Tip: You will want to remember when naming files to use underscore or hyphen connectors between words. Some Transfer Protocols (FTP) will not upload files with spaces in them and when they do, they put weird characters between the words.

To accomplish this task the steps are as follows.

Select File > Pack and Go. The Pack and Go Wizard starts. Click **Next**.

Pick the files to pack. Select **Active presentation** if your file is already open, or select **Other presentation(s)** to browse and select a file on your hard drive. Click **Next**.

Select a drive to copy the file to, by choosing a destination, and select a folder on your hard drive or storage medium in which to save the file. Click **Next**.

Select whether to include linked files and fonts in your packaged presentation file. You should always include linked files, and check the Embed TrueType fonts checkbox if you have any doubt whether the computer that will display the presentation has the required fonts. Click **Next**.

If there is a chance that the host computer may not have the PowerPoint program installed on it you will want to include the PowerPoint viewer. Select whether to include the Microsoft PowerPoint Viewer in your packaged file. Click **Next**.

Click **Finish**. PowerPoint creates two files— **PNGSETUP.EXE** and **PRES0.PPZ**. You need both files to show the packaged presentation. You can transfer them to portable media, such as a CD, DVD, or flash drive; send them via e-mail or FTP (File Transfer Protocol); or just take them with you if you saved them on your laptop computer. When you're ready to run the presentation, just **Run PNGSETUP.EXE**.

In PowerPoint 2007 the steps are just a bit easier to create an Autorun CD. This Autorun feature is one you may already be familiar with since it has been available in all PowerPoint versions since 2003. With all your images, audios, videos and slides in one neat folder follow these steps to prepare for transfer of your presentation to another computer.

Obviously, you will need a CD burner and a blank CD besides your files for your presentation.

Click the Window's Icon in the upper left of your PowerPoint screen. A dropdown menu appears. Now you will scroll down and select **Publish > Package for CD**.

Ignore the warning that pops up. It essentially lets you know that your presentation will be compatible with older PowerPoint software versions. Now you will see the **Package for CD** dialogue box. Simply give your presentation a name and move on to the next step by clicking on the **Add Files** button. Note that there is a limit of characters to your presentation's name so keep it as short as possible and avoid spaces between words.

As a word of warning: It is very important to the success of your presentation to have all your pieces in the same folder before creating your presentation. Unless all your files are in the same folder you will suffer the embarrassment of broken links in your presentation.

If you want to add more files to your CD this is the time to do that. However, the presentation that you are publishing is already active and part of the compilation. What this enables you to do is **Autorun** sequential presentations. If you only want the one you are currently working with to be embedded on the CD you can skip this step by selecting the **Options** button.

In the Options dialogue box you can select how your presentation will play. You can choose from four options. There are, in order,

- Play all presentations automatically in the specified order
- Play only the first presentation automatically
- Let the user select which presentation to view
- Don't play the CD automatically

If you select the last option, you or your viewer will have to manually open the presentation to view it thus disabling the **Autorun** feature.

In this dialogue box is where you will find the password protection feature. You can password protect the entire presentation or just the ability to edit it. Usually I like to password protect the editing of the presentation, but be sure you write the password down or you will cause yourself undue stress the next time you wish to change a word or edit your presentation in any way.

More information on this dialogue box can be found in the For Dummies book *Cutting Edge PowerPoint 2007* that I mentioned earlier.

When you have enabled all your options, choose **OK** to return to the Package for CD dialogue box.

The last step is to select the **Copy to CD** button. That's all there is to it. I suggest that once your CD is copied, you take a moment to open the CD to verify its contents.

Note: Flash drives can be used in place of the CD/DVD.

Dress for Success

What you wear is one of the most important decisions you will make. It will influence directly how you are perceived before even uttering your first word. **Wear something comfortable yet professional.** Of course, the venue will have a bearing on what you choose. Therefore, being familiar, or at least knowledgeable, of the venue prior to arrival is important. If you cannot visit the facilities ahead of time call your host to get the particulars.

If you are presenting out of doors, in the heat of the summer months, you will probably choose something light-weight with shorter sleeves. However, if your meeting is indoors in an auditorium you will probably want to wear something more conservative in nature. There are some key points that I would like to make here in regards to this issue.

First impressions are critical. Remember, you are marketing a product—yourself. If you want to command the respect of your audience, dress wisely. Short skirts, low cut blouses and tight clothing for the girls may be sexy but tend to be overly distracting to the audience. Men will be focused on you and not what you have to say and women will be offended to a point that you will lose them too.

Never, never, never, ever, show up looking unkempt! Be sure that whatever you choose is neatly pressed. If  you have been traveling and your clothes need pressing it is well worth the small investment to send your clothing out for pressing through the hotel pressing service. Contact your concierge or front desk for assistance. If you aren't going to be staying in a hotel that offers these services, I recommend highly that you pack and USE a travel iron. These wonderful little inventions are light-weight and usually compacted into a suitable carrying case. If you need to purchase one you will find them listed on eBay for anywhere between $3 and just over $20. Another good source is Amazon.com. As you would expect these items are higher priced, but you may also find that they are of better quality.

Here is a brief list of things you may want to consider.

Make sure you have

- Conservative dress shoes, clean and polished
- Neatly combed and styled hair
- Clean and manicured fingernails

Your hands will be a focal point for your audience as you will more than likely be using your hands to point out items, or perhaps, to highlight an important point. You probably will be simply standing with your fingertips together as you express or explain your ideas. When in this stance your hands will be in plain view of your audience. So, pay close attention to this seemingly minor detail of your appearance. Yes men, even you should consider having your fingernails professionally mani-cured. This doesn't mean you even have to wear a clear polish. There are ways to buff up the shine naturally that will give your hands a clean and neat look.

Use only minimal cologne or perfume, if any at all

You may want to refrain from wearing a scent as there may be audience members who have allergies that would be affected by the scent you choose. If you are in a small room that holds only a minimum number of participants this is something that deserves your consideration. If you are presenting to a small office staff you may want to check with your host/hostess as to any known problems for your attendees prior to your en-gagement.

No visible body piercing beyond conservative earrings

This goes for men as well as women. Unless you are speaking at a body piercing or tattoo seminar, stick with the conservative 'less is more' tradition.

Brushed teeth and fresh breath

Be sure to use dental floss. If you are lucky enough to present after lunch to your group, be sure that you take a moment to brush and floss prior to taking the stage. Also, if you love raw onions or garlic on your sandwich or salad this might be a good time to pass on these additions.

No gum, candy, or other objects in your mouth

When you are trying to make a good impression diction is important. Anything in your mouth that could hamper that diction is a no, no. That includes tongue piercings; especially if you aren't yet used to it. These are sure to cause slurring of words, so pull them out if you need to.

Also, as to gum, if you must chew gum throw it out prior to stepping to the podium and when chewing it, never chew it with your mouth even slightly open. This smacking sound is not only unbecoming and unprofessional but crass.

Minimal jewelry

When considering what jewelry you will wear remember that conservative dress is always best. You don't want to have your jewelry clanging and banging around. This will distract not only your audience, but may even throw you off. Remember, less is more.

Body odor

Little is needed to be said on this important topic. If you have a tendency to sweat profusely use a good antiperspirant and take a towel with you on stage.

Attire

Be sure to check your attire in the rest room just before your presentation for a final check of your appearance—to make sure your tie is straight; your hair is combed; etc.

In addition, the color you wear sends a clear message. Choose a neat, well-pressed suit or dress. Ladies, if your preferred attire is a dress, make sure that the hemline falls at or below the knee. Why you may ask, when you raise your arms to point or make expressive motions you, may not realize it but, your audience may be entitled to a view of you that you had no intention of sharing. I speak from experience here. This one little detail can save you years of embarrassment.

On the subject of hosiery, even in the heat of the summer in Florida I wear pantyhose when giving a presentation. Remember, your shoes should be conservative and close toed which lends well to the use of pantyhose. Red is a color that screams inappropriately. Unless you or your business is branded with that color, you would do better to choose something more subtle in shade. I am not saying you have to stick with the basic blues and blacks but consider the image you want to portray and the audience to whom you will be presenting.

For men the advice is to wear the classic 2- or 3-button suit. If you are presenting in a less formal venue you may consider wearing a sports jacket. The only recommendation here is to steer clear of the plaids or wild patterns. A blue or black suit coat is your better choice. You can always take the jacket off once you have taken the stage. Be sure your belt matches your shoes. *Ladies, your choice of shoe color should not reflect your blouse or belt; rather it should reflect your skirt or slacks color.* If you don't have a matching color, opt for a neutral shade.

A beard or mustache, it has been said, is considered a subtle statement that the wearer is hiding something. For that reason and that reason alone, erring on the side of conserva-

tism, I recommend that you remain clean-shaven if you intend to present a professional image. However, if you must wear facial hair it should be neatly combed and trimmed.

A very good friend of mine who is constantly in front of an audience of medical professionals explains it this way.

"You are better off choosing a dark suit, white or blue shirt, red or yellow tie. The fact is that a red or yellow tie is accepted as a power tie statement. It's bold and strong. If the speech is any good it projects a good man's image, but if the speech sucks he looks like a wannabe weenie."[1]

So what is the difference between **Corporate Casual** and **Business Casual**? Is there any difference at all? The answer is a resounding, "Yes." Corporate casual, as you might suspect, is just a hint more formal than business casual is. Apparel for corporate casual for men includes the long sleeve button collar shirt, which can be any color you choose, and well pressed, tailored slacks. The jacket and tie are optional. Whereas the business casual attire indicates long sleeve stripped or light blue unbuttoned or buttoned collar shirt and khaki slacks; again be sure your clothing is pressed and neat. Optionally you might choose to wear a company logoed long sleeve or polo style shirt with or without a sweater depending on the weather. Either way, make sure your shoes are clean and polished.

For the ladies, the difference in corporate casual and business casual is much the same, corporate casual being a tad more conservative than business casual. A corporate casual look for ladies entails a neatly pressed straight skirt usually worn with a conservative blouse. A scarf for accent may give you *la joie de vivre* that sets you apart. While the business casual attire can incorporate neatly pressed slacks as well as a looser flowing skirt with a stripped or printed top. Remember to keep your dress or skirt to a conservative length to save you from unnecessary embarrassment.

---

[1] Joe Cassels, Hospital Reps, Inc

Rehearse

I cannot stress enough the importance of practice. Practice with all of your props. Get comfortable with the handling of them. You wouldn't want to find, once you start, that the object you intend to use is too awkward to handle effectively and becomes more of a distraction than a help. Practice alone in front of a mirror and then when you are comfortable, ask a friend or family member to be your audience. If you have a video camera, you may want to record your presentation and review it. Be ready for what you will see and hear. Here are some things to take special note of while reviewing your video practice session.

- Look for rough spots that need a little more practice
- Be aware or the vocal pauses. Words like "uh" and especially "um."
- How you handle your visuals. Are you confident and sure or fumbling with them?
- Are you reading your slides or presenting to your audience?

Even more important to practicing your presentation, is to know your subject matter. The last thing you want to do is offer the wrong advice or misinformation. Making statements that are inaccurate will alienate the more knowledgeable people in your audience and can cause them to ignore or discount your entire presentation.

A good example of that would be the statement "Brushing your teeth doesn't prevent tooth decay." As with this statement, **if you are making a statement that people tend to discount as false, you need to offer data and facts to back your words up.** When presenting facts have them clearly stated and reference their source. This will lend credibility to you and your statements.

Be prepared to offer not only your opinions but hard evidence as well. If you rely too heavily on charts and graphs, you may bore your audience to tears. Find a balance that provides significant credence to your statements without over-whelming them with data.

Here is a real life, current example of how to present your statement and confirming facts that my husband recently shared with me. For this example, we will use the current controversy of embryonic stem cell therapy vs. adult stem cell therapy for treatment of a multitude of human diseases.

In spite of misleading claims to the contrary embryonic stem cells have far more potential than adult stem cells.

This statement to the lay public may be perplexing because of their lack of expertise. The addition of the following statement would do much to document the position supporting embryonic stem cells.

The American Association for the Advancement of Science (AAAS), the world's largest general scientific society, in testimony before the US Senate and in a letter to President Bush on July 18, 2006, testified in the US Senate that, "While all avenues of stem cell research should be explored, stem cells derived from early-stage human embryos appear by far to hold the greatest therapeutic promise." This information can be found on the AAAS website and in the Senate records.[2]

By this example, you can clearly see the way to properly present your facts without getting into off graphs and charts. However, if you need them do not hesitate to use them.

Be sure to pay close attention to the 'filler words' like "y'know," "um," "uh," etc. If you find yourself using them even once, concentrate on making yourself aware of them. Once you are aware of this presentational faux pas, you have come a long way in eliminating them.

Remember to tape your presentation for playback, so you can easily identify areas that need work. Whether that area is overuse of your movements, your 'filler words' or your overall flow, you will readily notice those problem areas when you review the tape and can concentrate on eliminating them.

Rehearsal of the transitions and the opening and closings will do more to boost your confidence level than anything else you rehearse. Practice with all of your tools as well as your notes and visuals. A highlighter pen comes in handy to pinpoint key words when you find yourself faltering.

You will want to try to **keep these notes to a minimum** so that you can easily pick up a word or two to remind you when you need a little nudge. Writing out your entire pre-sentation can be more confusing than helpful. The most annoying speeches are entirely scripted and sound choppy and unrehearsed.

Even the shortest talk, unrehearsed, or read word-for-word shows a lack of care. Inexperience speakers leave you feeling helpless to assist them as they communicate their message both choppily and with obvious nervousness in their voice. If you

---

[2] AAAS Letter to President George W. Bush
http://www.aaas.org/spp/cstc/docs/06_07_18stemcellBush.
pdf (accessed May 23, 2008).

learn nothing else about effective presentation, I hope you will always remember **to never, never, never read your presentation or slides**. You should be speaking to the audience and not to your slides.

There are only two instances when you should glance at your slide. They are to point to something on your slide or to watch for its appearance.

Becoming comfortable with your visual aids also takes practice. Here are some practical tips to ensure your presentation flows smoothly through the handling of them.

Get familiar with them

Practice handling your visuals until you can move smoothly from one to the next. You should be so familiar with the aids that you don't have to glance at them to remember your point.

Timing

Decide when you will introduce each item and when you will put it away. Don't pull props out until you're ready to use them and get rid of them as soon as you finish with them; otherwise, they can become a distraction. Also, consider distributing materials either before or after the presentation as opposed to during it.

Visuals are your friends not the other way around; Don't hide behind your materials. Their purpose is to enhance your message, not take the place of it.

Talk to the audience, not the aid: Keep eye contact with the audience. Show them to the audience not yourself.

Make sure your audience can see the visual aids: Stand aside, if necessary, or pass them around.

Pointing: Ignore what your mother told you about pointing and point to the visual aid or refer to it. This will let your audience know exactly which and even what part of the aid you are referencing.

Don't read them: Any visual aid that prompts you to read directly from it is a bad one. Visuals are used to clarify your point to your audience. They should never include the script of your speech. Remember, your audience came to see you not your slides. Use your visuals to fill their minds with an image and then fill the details in orally.

Use a metaphorical image rather than words and bullet points: This will ensure you will have your audience's full attention.

Give your audience time to assimilate

Give the audience a chance to see, and when applicable, touch. Pay close attention—is your audience absorbing the information you're presenting? Look for the non-verbal clues to help gauge your timing. Should you allow more time or less? If you see individual audience members looking askance or showing any body language signs that indicate that they are still processing the information pause and allow them to absorb the facts you have presented. Give additional examples if you feel the need. If you have supplied a workbook or study sheet suggest they refer to it at that time. Then pause and give them time to find the information you are referencing.

Never give a reference that you want them to look up without allowing this extra time. When you don't allow this time you will find them looking for the reference instead of paying attention to what you are saying.

Explain it to them

Even if you've done an outstanding job creating visuals that get the point across in an instant, your audience will grasp your point better when you explain your message to them.

If you find your presentation is too short or long you may be able to adjust simply by slowing down or speeding up the timing.

However, sometimes while I am practicing, I come to realize that the problem of timing can only be corrected by eliminating some of the fluff. Rarely, if ever, is it a problem of not having enough information to relay. However, that can also be a problem. If your host or hostess expects you to speak for twenty minutes and you only have ten minutes of information to present but don't realize that until you are halfway through your presentation there is no way to stretch your presentation enough to fill the gap. It is better to find this out during your rehearsal phase than during the presentation.

On the other hand, be prepared to shorten your presentation at a moment's notice. If and when this happens, this is not the time to focus on the negative of having your time cut short at the last minute, or you won't have time to think about what and where to cut. Having an idea and having practiced ahead of time can eliminate the last minute frustrations and worry of how to present an abbreviated version of your presentation. It does happen where due to time constraints you may be asked to make these modifications at the last minute. So, be ready and willing to be accommodating and you may just get asked back.

A Note on Notes

The choice is yours. You may find that printing your notes on paper is the easiest way to create them. However, printed sheets lend to over use.

Consider using note cards. They will help you focus on points and not lend to a completely scripted speech. Remember your notes should be just that; a reminder of the upcoming point or outline topic. Don't forget to number them. As mentioned earlier, this seemingly insignificant step could potentially save you from embarrassment should they fall to the floor.

Making a note of the amount of time it takes to get through each card or page will help you gauge whether your presentation is going to fill the time you have for your presentation. If while you are presenting you see that you are finishing at a different pace than when you practiced you can slow down or speed up as necessary. You may even have to eliminate whole sections of your speech at times to keep the presentation on schedule.

A good friend of mine recently told of a time when she was asked to present for half an hour to a very large audience as a lead-in to the keynote speaker. She dutifully prepared and rehearsed. On the day of the event, as she was standing in the wings waiting to present, the speaker before her ran well over her time. To eliminate the keynote speaker's address or shorten it was out of the question. So, what did the host do but ask my friend to cut her speech in half.

Realize she had put together all of her notes and slides and at this point had no way to communicate with the technical crew which slides to eliminate. Since she is a consummate professional, she was able to significantly shorten her presentation even under these circumstances by offering less information about each of her slides.

This is not a typical issue that you will run across but it can and does occur. So as I mentioned earlier, know your material and where you can shorten it and where you can't ahead of time. This will help you if and when this challenge develops.

The Next Generation: The Online Presentation Environment

In today's fast paced, ever changing technological environment the presentation is no longer limited to on-site performance. The Internet has exploded with opportunities to bring the whole world to your doorstep. Where we used to have simple one-on-one chat capability we now have unlimited capacity to reach out to all parts of the globe at the same time. You can literally give a global conference with slides, audio, and video from the comfort of your home.

For those of you who are in the direct selling market as well as the entrepreneur this means the world is your platform. Learning how to put these tools to good use is imperative to the expansion and success of your business.

At the expense of a friend's presentation, I offer this tip on presenting online demonstrations in the new Audio/Video

(A/V) Internet chat room environment. She had practiced her video presentation. What she saw on her monitor was functioning properly so she thought that what she had prepared was viewable by the other attendees. Unbeknownst to her, due to the encryption of the website she was presenting, her attendee's monitors were not bringing up the same site information she was seeing. This left her flustered and groping to come up with a quick solution.

The point I am making here is that not only should you practice your presentation to ensure that you can properly see all of your slides and access all your pages, but have a friend on another computer be your practice audience. Sometimes you can see the presentation and access all the slides and websites you wish to display, but what your audience receives on their computer may be either blocked or not accessible.

Here also it is a good option to have a monitor working with you as you present. Unless you are very familiar with the software you are using in the A/V environment the assistance of a monitor, who is familiar with the environment, can significantly affect how your audience perceives your professionalism.

New online presentational software companies crop up every day. They all have different ways of enabling you to use this rapidly developing medium. Some A/V environment providers offer a quick course in the use of the equipment and back room tools. I highly recommend that you take the time to familiarize yourself with them by going through this brief introduction. If you don't have the time to attend the training, have

No matter which AV chat room you decide to use be sure it is both MAC and PC friendly. If is also supports Linux so much the better.

someone you know who will be able to assist should difficulties crop up, as you can be sure they will, go through it for you, or hire the room monitor if they provide one. This is a minor expense but well worth the money spent if and when you need their expertise.

If you are investing in the software for your company for presentations, seminars, or collaborations taking the tutorial tour or practicing ahead of time will give you the familiarity and confidence you need to successfully present your material.

One such environment is the Hot Conference Room. This type of room provides a window where everyone views the information presented.

What you will see when you open a Hot Conference room is a window, usually on the left with a list of the attendees. For familiarity sake and building what is known as the "know, like and trust" factor I highly recommend you always use your full

name when logging into the A/V conference room environment.

Underneath the roster you will see a box that allows the speaker to upload a static image of them-selves or enable live video image for those who have a webcam installed and enabled on their computer system.

Directly under that you will find the communication controls, the speaker volume and microphone toggle switch. There are three ways to enable the attendees to hear you when you speak. The easiest way is to left mouse click and hold the talk button directly under the control switches. However, there are times when you will want to use one of the other two methods. The first of these methods is available to all attendees. You can set up a HotKey or if you are signed in as a moderator you will see a box next to the Talk Now button that when clicked will lock the talk button into the on position.

Directly adjacent to these left screen areas you will find a large display window. This is where the presenter will display the URL of the topical discussion. Below this is where messages you type will be displayed. If a person wants to privately message a specific individual to the right of the text input area below the text display box is a drop down list of all attendees. Select the name of the person you wish to private message to and type away. However one word of caution here, when you want to go back to text messaging the entire group you will have to clear the 'private to' name.

Most A/V rooms now have the ability to use what is known as an 'annotation' tool. This can also be used with a 'whiteboard' if you need a clean white sheet for presenting.

The annotation tool usually offers the ability to type and highlight as well as drawing lines to point to items or encase your text in shapes to bring attention to a specific area or point on your slide. Being familiar with how annotation tools work may add the punch to your presentation that otherwise would be missing.

Another type of A/V room you will find is Desktop Sharing. Some Hot Conference rooms are beginning to see the benefit of using this type of forum and are adding it to their software. Desktop sharing allows the speaker to enable the viewer to see what the presenter is seeing on their desktop. The attendees as viewers are able to follow along with the host or presenter as the information is shared directly from the speaker's computer. There are many of these types around and they are gaining popularity among the speaking community.

One huge benefit is less reliance on the A/V room. No longer do you need to upload your presentation to the room for display. Rather you merely bring it up on your computer and then allow your attendees to follow along as you progress through your slides.

Another use that many companies are finding for this Desktop Sharing technology is the ability to collaborate. This means you enable more than one attendee to share the mouse and control the host computer. When colleagues meet in this environment a lot can be accomplished in a very short time. This is especially useful for companies who have employees that work in different locations.

With Desktop sharing capability the audio portion of the collaboration is done via a conference line. These numbers are usually offered by the provider of the software and often are reusable for a full month.

One other option you might consider is the use of Skype. Skype is a downloadable program that enables Instant Messaging (IM). It is free to use and has many add-ins that increase its functionality.

With Skype you can chat via text or voice. They offer conferencing capability for group discussions and interface with software that allows you to record the vocal part of the conversation as well as desktop share to name a few.

In a recent church service Skype was used effectively to conference with a missionary family in Chili, live. Even in 2010 the video/audio portion didn't quite sync, but actually talking and speaking real-time with them made the transfer of information much, much simpler.

For a short-list of available A/V software check the Resource Section located in the final pages of this book.

The Do's and Don'ts of Presenting

What you do and don't do during your public speaking event will directly influence your audience's responsiveness.

The thought of your first presentation may be a bit worrisome. Nevertheless, as you become comfortable with speaking in front of an audience, you may decide that the use of a podium is unnecessary. When that time comes, remove it. This will allow you to move around freely and creates a more intimate setting. While getting to that comfort level will take time, be assured you will get there. Until then, using a podium will not only give you a place to hold your notes, but will help to establish you as a person worthy of attention.

Presentational skills are a practiced art. Every actor, whether on stage or screen, knows this. Poise and tone of voice do a lot to enhance your credibility. Your delivery should be clear and easy to understand. Enunciating your words while remaining natural and believable conveys genuine emotion as opposed to coming off forced or scripted.

It has often been said speak just above a whisper if you want to be heard. However, when presenting you will find that both loud and clear and soft and intimate are effective in their own times. Be careful with the volume; don't overwhelm the room or you'll run the risk of offending your audience.

Variation in both speed and volume can work wonders. They help you to convey different messages. For example, talking quickly conveys excitement and energy, but can easily grate and annoy if you do it for too long or too often. Likewise, talking slowly can help complex ideas or very important points go down more smoothly, however after a while it can lull your audience to sleep. So, variety is the key in this case.

Some of us have significantly developed vocal chords while others need direction in this area. As a soloist, I find that more often than not I need to tone down the volume rather than pump it up. My husband has even gone so far as to accuse me of yelling at him when I was talking in my normal voice. When he is right behind me and I believe him to be in another room that statement is understood. If you also have a strong voice, accept that fact and learn to control it.

On the other hand, if you have a soft voice or it tires easily you may want to seek the advice of a professional coach. A voice coach can train you to vocalize properly. With proper technique and training you can significantly strengthen your vocal muscles. **A tip like warming up your vocal chords is not good advice just for singers.** Anyone who uses their voice to project any distance should go through warm up exercises. One that I have found particularly helpful is to simply hum to myself. The tune need not even be to a real song, perhaps you might just want to find a note, vocalize it for a few seconds, and then try to reach one just a bit higher or lower. Some may prefer to run the scales or sing aloud. Whatever your preference, warming up your voice prior to speaking is an exercise I highly recommend.

With the assistance and direction of a Vocal Coach you can you learn how to control your voice, your breathing, and you diction too. A thorough knowledge of vocal techniques will come in mighty handy throughout your career as a professional speaker. This is an investment in yourself and your business and one that is well worth the time and money.

To find a coach in your area you may want to check the music or drama department of your local college. Some churches have professional music department personnel that can be of assistance in this area as well. For vocal coaches that I recommend that you see the Resource Section. In addition, you will find a couple of books that you may find useful.

Body Language

Non-verbal communication is the art of employing body language to better gauge how effectively you communicate with others. This form of communication happens whether you intend to use it or not. Every day we send out non-verbal clues to those around us. Employing just a few simple techniques can reinforce the message you are trying to convey. Therefore, learning how to identify and use this powerful language will do much to enhance your speaking ability.

Eye contact and gestures are forms of body language that every speaker quickly learns to employ. Looking your audience in the eye conveys to them not only you are genuine but also that what you have to say is worth hearing. Maintaining good eye contact, when first meeting others, shows respect and interest. Try to keep your eye contact to about 60-70% of the time you are speaking with a person for the first time. Be careful not to overdo it or stare as this implies intensity and is often offensive. On the contrary, very little eye contact indicates shyness and lack of confidence.

71

Leaning towards the audience indicates interest. Remember, you have an entire room of eyes to choose from. Look around the room. Try to make eye contact with several members of your audience not just one or two. Keep your eyes on the audience—not the clock.

If you are too nervous to actually look your audience in the eye, try looking just above their heads. Focus on giving the sense that you are looking at them and not through them.

Your face is the most expressive part of your body. Smile genuinely and often. This simple act will help you appear warm, open, interested, friendly and most of all confident.

Gestures can also be effective tools to enhance a point. However, don't over use them or you might be conceived as nervous and ill prepared or flamboyant and fake. Have you ever been sitting with someone, changed your position slightly, and noticed that the person sitting with you changed his or her position to match yours? This is body language communication at its best. When they conform to your position, they are telling you that they agree with you and trust what you are saying to be true. This is the type of response you should strive to achieve with your audience. However, since you cannot sit with them, nor should you unless you have a physical need to, you must employ this concept with your gestures and stance.

Watch your audience for clues. When they touch their cheek or chin, or tilt their head, they are subconsciously telling you that they are contemplating and digesting what you are telling them. The tilted head is an indication of a question so give them time to digest. If their touching includes rubbing, such as their rubbing of their nose or eyes this could be an indication of anything from disbelief to rejection or doubt.

Are they sitting with arms crossed in front of them in a defensive posture or with their hands in their lap? These are also indications that there are accepting or rejecting what you are saying. Perhaps you need to add a bit more clarity to your point. Remember that not everyone will agree with you so don't over inform or try to convince the entire audience. Simply state your case and give them time to absorb your content.

If you see that your audience is sitting with their legs crossed swinging their leg this is an indication of boredom. To change this you could either pull them in to your presentation or wrap it up. This can be done in numerous ways. You could ask them a question and that would allow them to participate in the discussion or perhaps you might simply stop and ask them to stand and stretch, especially if your presentation has been a lengthy one.

Posture is the most important of all body languages. Have you ever seen an important person portrayed as slouched and slovenly? On the contrary, they stand tall and present a commanding demeanor. One of the simplest ways of letting your audience know that you are in control and worthy of their time is to walk and talk with the air of authority. This is not to say you should become pious. There is a fine line here, be careful not to cross it. Standing straight while remaining natural will portray a genuineness as well as authority.

By all mean, **keep your hands out of your pockets!** If you find your hands are getting in the way simply hold them in front of you with your thumbs and first two fingers touching each other with the opposite hand forming a triangle. I am certain you have noticed professional speakers in this stance. Alternately, you can let them fall comfortably at your sides. Some presenters disagree, and in a small group may be effective; but to me it is unprofessional.

Absolutely do not play with your hair or tug at your clothing. These gestures can convey to your audience that you are insecure and lack self-confidence. For the ladies, you may not realize it but your hairstyle itself makes a definite statement. You may be aware that a well groomed hairstyle portrays a professional appearance while unkempt hair is a sure way of stating your obvious lack of commitment not only to yourself but your audience and message as well. Additionally, when presenting professionally you may find that long hair is best pinned up for more reasons than one. It not only is a neat and professional look, but it keeps it out of your eyes and face thus allowing you to concentrate on your presentation rather than your appearance.

All of these tools are at your disposal if you just learn how to read and use them properly. Not only can you use them when offering your presentation but you can make even better use of them in the meet and greet time before or after your presentation as well as in your daily lives.

Speaking of the meet and greet time a word to the wise when shaking hands upon first meeting someone new be aware of the message your handshake delivers. When delivering your hand for the handshake I recommend that you present it upright and vertical. This may seem silly to mention to some but the hand extended palm side down indicates dominance or aggressiveness and may be seen as offensive to the receiver. Also, if you want to portray a real genuine interest in what is being said verbally you might find yourself covering the handshake with your other hand.

Additionally, don't stand too close. We all have our comfort area. The 'zone' that we consider off-limits to strangers. Unless you are invited into that intimate area, refrain from breaking that barrier. This is not to say that you cannot touch the arm of the person you are meeting, just be aware of their comfort level. Touching indicates a level of trust or bonding by both parties so be careful not to overstep these bounds if you are not invited in.

Perhaps simply leaning in their direction may be all that is called for. As mentioned earlier this leaning towards the other person is a way to indicate that you are interested in what they have to say. If you think you are a bit too far away and take a step closer to them and they take a step back, realize that you have intruded on their *private space*. Pay attention here if you wish not to risk becoming over aggressive or intrusive.

Let me say here that body language is not an exact science so take it in context. For example, if someone is rubbing their nose it could be an indication that they have a cold and not that they doubt what you are telling them to be true.

There are numerous books available on this subject. Check your local library or book retailer for books on this subject. One that I have found informative and helpful I have listed in the Resource Section.

Manage your fear

Fear is real. It can stop you in your tracks. Whether founded or unfounded the fact is fear is a part of our animal instinct. Fear of the unknown, fear of danger, and the fear you experience when you are faced with the knowledge that you have to put yourself in front of an audience where you will be judged worthy or unworthy of their attention are all real and tangible fears.

What are you afraid of? When you are asked to say a few words to a crowded room does your throat go dry and your knees begin to knock? Do you experience a tingling in your entire body? Or a constricting in your stomach?

You are not alone. No matter how real or imagined your fear seems the paralyzing fear of stage fright is manageable.

Truly, there are only three ways to manage your fear.
Confront it

Embrace your fear. Look it straight in the eye. Analyze it. Ask yourself, "Why am I afraid?" Figure it out for yourself. What is it that is causing your fear? Then deal with it.

Use it

Realize that fear is a tool. Stage fright is your friend. I know that this sentence may not sit well with you, but in reality it is a truth that you need to embrace.

After more than 45 years of being on a stage either singing, acting or presenting I find that every time I confidently take the stage I am struck by a case of nerves up until I get *in the flow*. A while back, I was asked at the last minute to step in and perform a solo at a function. With no notice, I took the stage and presented a rendition of a song that I knew well, but had not rehearsed for quite some time. I remember vividly my legs shaking so badly that I had to change my stance several times. However, only I knew how nervous I really was. Afterwards I was complimented and even nodded approval as I took my seat.

This thing we call stage fright is what keeps us keenly aware that we are seeking approval. Your audience not only wants you to succeed, but they are silently sending forth their positive energy to encourage you.

Let go of it

A mere seven seconds after you take the stage you have set the attitude for your entire presentation. To ensure your acceptance be genuine in your delivery. Remember to thank your host or hostess, by name, for inviting you. Don't expect to enthrall each and everyone in your audience. But do acknowledge them with a glance around the room and don't focus on just one person in the audience. Share your attention and acknowledgements evenly.

I have been told to look at a spot on the wall, but I think that is inconsiderate of your audience. If you can get past the fear that grips you at the start, make eye contact with your audience.

One suggestion I would like to share is prior to your event meet and greet some of the attendees. Do your best to address them by name. This takes paying attention to them and not thinking ahead to your presentation. This will go a long way to win your audience over and make them feel important. As you greet them, you may also want to reassess your message to better fit your audience. A simple anecdote about someone you just met or sharing some other personalized tidbit you've just gleaned from among them creates a rapport with your audience faster than anything else you could offer. These sorts of personal touches show groups that you not only understand them but you were also listening.

Things to remember
Avoid slang

Try not to use abridged or informal variations of words and phrases. You run the risk of ostracizing yourself and making the audience deem you as lazy or sloppy. This use of slang or the lack thereof should be kept in mind whether your presentation is aural or written. Even authors and those who are advice givers from every walk of life need to adhere to this rule. Imagine using a colloquialism that you are familiar with only to receive back blank stares from your audience who has no clue what you just said.

Better to leave them out altogether than to ostracize your audience.

Eliminate verbal fillers

Avoid peppering your sentences with "ums," "ahs," and other words that serve no good purpose. They tell your audience you are uncomfortable, at the least, unprofessional and not worthy of their full attention, at worst.

Don't hide your hands

Keeping your hands in your pockets or behind your back conveys a level of shiftiness to the viewer. If you want people to trust you, keep your hands where they can see them.

Do be on time

Better yet, be early. This is a quick way to gain the respect of your host or hostess. It tells them that you respect them enough to arrive on time. It further enables you to survey the room and check the equipment to ensure it is functioning correctly, besides being a valuable meet and greet time. Be sure to take a few moments just prior to your presentation in a quiet

place away from the crowd. This not only allows you to pull your thoughts together, but is a clear statement to your audience that you are a genuine professional.

Clear your throat

If you have a scratchy throat and need to clear it, explain this to your audi-

ence. A sip from that bottled water you packed to bring along will be helpful at this juncture.

Show enthusiasm

This will help to get your audience excited about your presentation. Remember, enthusiasm is contagious.

The Presentation

You are now ready to present. You have arrived at the venue early enough to check the available equipment and are prepared for any unfortunate event that might disrupt your presentation, i.e., a burnt out projector bulb, seating arrangements and such.

You have met with, assessed your audience, and know how you will inspire them by including them in your presentation, if you can.

You are standing at the podium or on the stage with your audience awaiting your opening. How do you make this transition? What do you do or say next?

As I mentioned before, begin by thanking your host or hostess for inviting you. Be sure to mention them by name. If your host or hostess has not already introduced you, share that information now. If they have, you might share a little personal information about yourself. Remember, they are here ready and willing to listen to you and what you have to say. They are actually seeking your advice and hoping to learn something valuable. They **WANT** you to succeed!

When in New York one of the quickest ways to generate a cheer of approval is to shout, "I Love New York!" There is a reason for that. Use that knowledge to your advantage. Break the ice before going into your presentation.

There are several ways to **'break the ice'** that speakers of all levels have used to their advantage. The first and most commonly used icebreaker is an anecdote or personal story. Give them something to relate to you with, begin by sharing.

Another oft-used icebreaker is to tell a joke. Nothing breaks the ice quicker than making your audience laugh. It gets their attention and prepares them for your message by helping you connect with them; that will help you make a positive impression.

A word of warning if your joke is completely off-topic it can further distance you from your audience. Pegging your jokes to either your audience or your subject will make them much more relevant and hence, funnier.

It goes without saying: Telling a sexist or racist joke will get people's attention, but won't necessarily engender a positive response. Avoid them at all costs.

Throughout your presentation, to break things up a bit, humor can be useful. A funny story may assist you in illustrating an important point.

Practice your jokes

Delivery can make or break it. If you are like me and can't tell a joke to save your life, **DON'T** (no exceptions!). My attempts at humor just come off as lame. If jokes are not your cup of tea, realize it and accept it. Know that there are other ways to break the ice that are much better for you to use than joke telling.

In a small group setting, the 'guess who' game may be a good way to start things rolling. This is when you have your audience or a portion of them share a moment in their life that others may not be aware. Have them write it on a sheet of paper and then hand them to you. As you read them, everyone tries to guess to whom the event belongs.

I use variations of this one and always get at least one funny and unique answer. One woman told me once that she had kissed a moose on her front porch and another time it was shared that the person, as a child, had stolen all the peanuts that had been hidden for a party because she had not been invited. She ended up getting caught while consuming the evidence.

Even in a corporate business setting, or perhaps especially in that setting, your audience is often seeking a break from the stoic business meeting. Jumping immediately into the presentation without taking the time to 'break the ice' first is what that audience has come to expect. If you want to really make an impression take the time to incorporate a moment of genuine sharing before plodding ahead.

Remember the first rule of icebreakers, 'involve the audience.'

Command Performance

The audience is in place and you have stepped up to the podium or onto the stage. You've broken the ice; this is your time to shine. As you begin, one of the first things you have to do is present yourself well. You are here for a reason. People are waiting to hear what you have to say because **you are the expert**. It is much easier to present yourself as an expert if you act like one. Be careful you don't overdo it and come off as a *know-it-all*.

Instead of naming all your accomplishments and degrees let your presentation and the way you hold yourself speak for you. Know your facts, and deliver them well. Provide them with the proof to back up your words within your presentation. You want them nodding and learning not dozing. If you aren't convincing as an expert in the field, present the facts and figures and name the source, especially if the source is a recognizable authority.

Make sure your audience is on the same page with you. Open your presentation with a summary of what you will be covering. Perhaps just a sentence or two to let them know what your topic will be and what you wish to accomplish. This will not only give them an idea of what they will get out of your presentation but it will help them to better grasp the key points when you get to them.

If your presentation is an informative presentation meant to teach them, let them know. Give them time to absorb the material before going on to the next subject. However, if your presentation is more of the persuasive type your job will be to persuade  them and ease them into your way of thinking on the subject matter.

When presenting a persuasive speak your job is to **answer the five 'W's**; who, what, where, when and why. You might want to begin by stating the problem or question and then briefly suggest who is affected by it and what you wish to prove. Stating your facts clearly and with conviction will assist you in establishing your position of authority.

Now that your audience is properly informed as to what is in store it is time to begin your presentation. Don't forget to smoothly transition between your opening and your actual presentation.

Remember that what you want to present is a professional, well thought-out, production. This is where a good outline will come in handy. While your outline should be just that, a means of jogging your memory about what you want to touch on next, your actual facts-and-figures and even quotes should be fully written out. The last thing you want to do is offer incorrect information or quotes. You might get lucky and no one will notice the mistake, but chances are there will be at least one person in your audience that will know better. You may even want to write those out in full in the handouts that you have prepared.

Your aim is to keep a *'conversational flow'*. Avoid reading your presentation word for word except for those facts-and-figures and direct quotes.

If you lose your place just keep going. You can always go back and pick up missed information later, if you need to. Another point I would like to make here is that if you wouldn't normally hear the words you want to use in conversation, don't use them. In other words, leave out the *'big words'* unless of course you are speaking on a technical subject that would be better accepted with their inclusion. And then, make sure you know how to pronounce them properly. Remember that your audience makeup will also determine if and when you should use these technical or *big words*. If you are addressing an audience of technically or scientifically educated people then your choice of words will be much different than if you are addressing a group of children. Adjust your language accordingly.

One way you can endear your audience and gain their attention and respect is to include them in your presentation. You might mention one of the attendees you met before your presentation by name while making a point. Yet another way is to simply ask them for a show of hands. You might try asking them something about their personal lives that has a bearing on your subject. For example if you are presenting, as I have in the past, on financial matters you might ask something like:

"How many of you have children or grandchildren?"

"How many of you here would rather be at the beach?"

This last question almost always generates a more relaxed atmosphere quicker than any other I have used. Of course, most often your questions should be based on your topic, but that should give you some idea of how you can use a question to generate action and interest.

Yet another means to draw your audience into the conversation is to pose a question that you know will generate answers that you intend to discuss. Make a note of pertinent suggestions if you can on a white board or flip chart. These are the suggestions that will parallel topics you already plan to discuss. Touching on them throughout the presentation gives the audience a personal stake in what you have to say.

When you have a long presentation scheduled or are participating in a conference or workshop you should make use of breaks. I tend to get sleepy after lunch—remembering that fact is important. Why? Because if you plan your presentation delivery after a lunch or dinner break you need to be extra careful not to lull the audience to sleep with a long, tedious dissertation or a darkened room as with video presentations. You might want to open with something exciting or energizing. Maybe even just having them all stand in place and stretch will do the trick.

Alternately, when resuming your presentation after a break, don't just dig into the meat of the matter unless your time is limited. Start with another icebreaker. You might transition with a statement about the lunch itself if you shared it together.

This would also be a good time to share a visual aid, pass around an object that has a bearing on your presentation or simply present it. Always introduce your audience to your object. This will help your listeners to better understand the connection between your words and your visual aid. Make a simple statement like, "As we look at this...".

Using visual aids as transitional tools can provide the perfect link between subjects. You need to be clear about what you have brought to share and why and how it fits with what you have to say. Handle them expertly; never read your slides or your visual aid and refrain from turning your back to the audience, if at all possible.

Working With A/Vs

Audio/Visual aids can make a powerful impact when used correctly. However, when used improperly, mishandled, or even just the lack of knowledge in the handling of them can be costly to your overall presentation. Be careful that you know not only what materials you are using but how to use them.

If you are not sufficiently familiar with the equipment to correct minor technical errors, you will want to have someone who can assist you. Their presence alone, when you need them, will garner respect and they can take control should the need arise.

Take the time to arrive early enough to ensure that the equipment is properly set up. This includes checking the focus and volume. Having to fiddle with minor adjustments tells your audience that you were not properly prepared and that they weren't worth the effort to arrive early enough to make certain that your equipment was fully operational.

No matter how many times you have rehearsed with your A/V presentation, act as if it is the first time you ever saw it. Your audience will note your enthusiasm or lack of it. This is not a license for sloppiness, merely a cue to keep the excitement alive in your speaking manner.

When presenting a slide show presentation you should consider how you are going to manage the slide advances. If you have your presentation timing down you can automate this process. When you want to take a little extra time to discuss one of the slides you can always interrupt the preset timing and restart it when you are ready to move on.

Physically, either you can have someone handle the slide changer or you could employ the mouse functions to advance your sides yourself. However, if you really want to provide the smoothest transition you may want to **invest in a special USB (universal serial bus) pointing device** to click through slides manually.

When it comes to your handouts, you will need to decide whether to give them out ahead of time or hold them for distribution as the attendees depart. If the handout is meant to be referred to during the presentation, by all means, give it out before. A handout that is filled with more than just reference material should be given out after your presentation. As stated earlier, giving out these types of packets prior to your presentation can serve as a distraction to your audience members.

I recall a time when the pastor of my church left the order of service entirely out of the bulletin. Not only were the church members more attentive that week, but the flow of the service was presented in such a manner that he was able to retain the attention of the congregation.

When handing out physical objects give the audience time to handle them. It may be wise to pause and reflect or review during this time because your attendees' attention will be disrupted until the object has completed its rounds. If the audience is overly large, you may want to simply show it or have several of the same article available to pass out from different parts of the room.

Once you are done with a physical object put it away; an unnecessary object left out and visible remains a source of distraction.

In this chapter, we touched on several important presentational elements. We discussed the importance of familiarity in the use and handling of your audio/visual aids—knowing when to pull them out and when to put them away. We found that this familiarity is not limited to physical objects.

We also learned that knowing your venue, or having someone present who does, is imperative—and to always show up early.

Now we are ready to tackle the all-important close.

The Close

Your presentation is nearing its end. You have covered all your *key points* and presented the *facts-and-figures* to corroborate your views.

Finally, we will discuss one of the most important aspects of your presentation—how to effectively and efficiently end your presentation. We will discover how to leave your audience with a positive impression and how to use materials to reinforce your message well after the presentation is over.

The best way to close is quickly, but not abruptly. Short and sweet are the words that come to mind. One simple phrase that will assist you in the transition from main body to your close might be, "In conclusion..." That succinctly informs your audience that you have completed your presentation. After that, you will probably want to offer a summary of your key points and finally leave them with something to ponder or a call to action depending on your type of presentation.

One of the best ways to close with a punch is to offer a statistic or fact, something that you have already stated or even one additional item. You might want to simply offer a quote from an expert.

Remember, this is your last chance to convince your audience that what you have been talking about is important enough for them to remember and/or take action on.

Offer something that the attendees will deem valuable. It could be anything from a gift certificate or discount coupon to merely a CD/DVD copy of your presentation. Have a fishbowl at the back of the room and have the attendees drop their business card into it to receive your thank you gift. What better way to obtain all your attendees valuable contact information. If you don't want to foot the expense of the CD/DVDs and the time to create them, you might consider offering them a link where they can download it from YOUR website.

In your closing, **always provide your audience with a way to contact you for further information or questions**. Then close your presentation with a "thanks for coming." If they have been especially enjoyable to speak to, you might even ask them to give themselves a round of applause. People love praise and acknowledgement. This is always well received, and it will clearly establish the conclusion of your talk.

In direct sales, your close is what will make or break your business. Done effectively your closing rate will soar. If you want to try your new found presentational skills in this market or to obtain a list of all direct selling associations in the world visit Direct Selling Association, www.dsa.org.

If I can offer one last tidbit, it would be to relax! Chances are your audience will have fun if you do. Remember, they are rooting for you and want you to do a good job! So, prepare and practice and then **RELAX** and enjoy.

Resources

Disclaimer: If you make a purchase or use the services of any companies listed in this eBook, the author cannot be held responsible for the deliverability or reputation.

Resources

Audio/Video Rooms - shortlist

ChatBlazer—http://www.chatblazer.com

Hot Conference—http://www.hotconference.net

Instant Teleseminar—http://instantteleseminar.com

Ojeez—http://www.ojeez.com

Skype—http://www.Skype.com

Vyew—http://vyew.com

Yugma—http://www.yugma.com

AV/VA

Ray Barry—bbarry5@embarqmail.com

Charly Leetham—http://thekeys2internetmarketing.com/online-video-production

Misty Taggart—http://www.TrailerToTheStars.com

Books

Change Your Voice, Change Your Life by Dr. Morton Cooper—http://www.voice-doctor.com/bookchgvoice.htm

Cash In On Speaking by Felicia J. Slattery, M.A., M.Ad.Ed. Communication Consultant, Speaker & Coach—Available in eBook format at http://wahmcart.com/x.php?adminid=1859&id=3149

Cutting Edge PowerPoint for Dummies by Geetesh Bajaj—http://www.amazon.com/dp/0764598171

PowerPoint 2007 Complete Makeover Kit by Geetesh Bajaj and Echo Swinford—http://www.amazon.com/dp/B00142APBW

Resources

Teach Yourself VISUALLY PowerPoint 2010 by William Wood, Bill Wood— John Wiley & Sons (2010) - Paperback - 320 pages - ISBN 0470577665

The 3-Dimensional Voice by Joni Wilson— http://www.joniwilsonvoice.com/series.htm

The Definitive Book of Body Language by Barbara Pease and Allan Pease—http://www.amazon.com/dp/0553804723

Leadership Development, Vocal/Speaker & Media Coaches

Kristen Beireis—http://www.virtualhelper4u.com

Lisa Braithwaite—http://www.CoachLisaB.com

Joe Yazbeck, Prestige Leader Development— http://www.prestigeleader.com

Joe Yazbeck, President, Senior Coach, Heartbeat Productions Vocal and Performance Coaching— http://www.heartbeatproductionsinc.com

Reference Resources

Bartleby—http://www.Bartleby.com

Wikipedia—http://www.Wikipedia.com

Urban Dictionary—http://www.UrbanDictionary.com

Software

Power Finish, Studio F Productions— http://www.powerfinish.com/business-templates/id/805_1

Websites

Adobe—http://www.Adobe.com

Direct Selling Association—http://www.dsa.org

Ellen Finkelstein, PowerPoint MVP—
http://www.EllenFinkelstein.com

Reinhard Diestel's, Introduction to Graph Theory—
http://www.math.ubc.ca/~solymosi/443/GraphTheoryIII.pdf

Websites—Quotes

Woopidoo—http://www.Woopidoo.com

Quotations Page—http://www.QuotationsPage.com

LeadershipNow—
http://www.LeadershipNow.com/quotes.html

The Quote Garden—http://www.quotegarden.com

About the Author

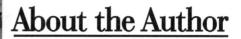

Ginger Carter-Marks is the owner of two successful writing and design companies, DocUmeant and DocUmeantDesigns. She has been assisting business owners of all sizes, from the personal business owner to the major fortune 500 companies, for over 30 years.

Her written works have been published in both print and digital mediums. Further, she enables authors to realize their dreams of self-publishing through her New York City based publishing company, DocUmeant Publishing.

Mrs. Marks has written several articles, reports, books, and eBooks. She also authors a monthly ezine titled Words of Wisdom, all of which are available through her main business site DocUmeant. http://www.documeant.net/. Her annual book series titled, *The Weird & Wacky Holiday Marketing Guide* is a look into how to use unusual holidays to market your business, and is available at HolidayMarketingGuide.com in eBook format, as well as, quarterly, rebrandable booklets.

Additional Titles by Ginger

Complete Library of Entrepreneurial Wisdom
http://www.CLEWbook.com (2013)
ISBN: 978-1-9378013-8-0

Weird & Wacky Holiday Marketing Guide, Your Calendar of
Business Marketing Ideas (Annual Editions since 2009)
http://www.HolidayMarketingGuide.com
ISBN13: 978-0-9826005-7-3

Back to Basics (2006)

Ten Truths of Business Ownership (2008)

How to Create Success—Free eBook
http://www.documeant.net/gingermarks.php

Ezine Articles Diamond Level Expert Author
http://ezinearticles.com/?expert=Ginger_Marks

Words of Wisdom ezine
http://www.documeantdesigns.com/

The complete line of reports and titles by Ginger Marks is available at
http://www.GingerMarksBooks.com

www.ingramcontent.com/pod-product-compliance
Lightning Source LLC
Chambersburg PA
CBHW051252050326
40689CB00007B/1171